THE ESSENTIAL GUIDE TO
SCOTTISH DANCING

Let's have a
Ceilidh

ROBBIE SHEPHERD

MUSIC SELECTED AND ARRANGED BY
JIM JOHNSTONE

CANONGATE PRESS

Dedicated to my wife Esma,
son Gordon and Mum
(with memories of Dad)

First published in Great Britain in 1992 by
Canongate Press
14 Frederick Street
Edinburgh EH2 2HB

British Library Cataloguing-in-Publication Data
A catalogue record for this book is available on request
from the British Library.

ISBN 0 86241 412 1

Phototypset by Hewer Text Composition Services,
Edinburgh
Printed and bound in Great Britain by
BPCC Hazells Ltd
Member of BPCC Ltd

Acknowledgments

And here's a hand my trusty fiere
And gie's a hand o' thine!
Auld Lang Syne

Yes, I do indeed most heartily extend the hand of friendship and gratitude to all those who have made this book possible. In particular I express my sincere appreciation to four folk all well known in the Scottish dance music scene who have helped me try to break down the stuffiness and technical jargon and present a beginner's guide and a teacher's revision course covering some of our most popular ceilidh and old-time dances.

Jim Johnstone has selected and arranged the music for the dances and unlike the majority of the set dances in the publications of the Royal Scottish Country Dance Society, most of the dances here do not have what is termed an 'original' tune for the dance. I am very grateful to Jim then for his choice of music, reflecting the tunes he finds most popular and most fitting to the particular dance. It may not be everyone's choice but I can guarantee you this, it fits the dance and it makes the ceilidh! Well, our man of music needs no introduction to Scotland's dancing public. He was born into the scene with his father and uncles already playing in dance bands in the Lothians. Jim himself first broadcast at the age of thirteen and formed his own band a couple of years later. He played with Jimmy Shand on and off for a number of years and the mutual respect remains to this day.

In writing about the background to the dances, amongst the books I consulted were *Traditional Dancing in Scotland* by J. P. and T. M. Flett (Routledge and Kegan Paul, London) and *Music and Society in Lowland Scotland in the Eighteenth Century* (Oxford University Press). These

I can heartily recommend for a cauld winter's nicht by the fireside when there's not a dance on the go!

For the dance instruction, I sought out the expertise of two ladies from different parts of the country who have in the past accepted my invitation on to numerous dancefloors—not because I was the expert—but because I knew they would guide me round in spite of my inadequacies. The first lady is Margaret Smith of Newtongrange and indeed a fine partnership has been built up in the last seven or eight years with Jim supplying the music to Margaret's dances and dance classes. The second is Marlene Lowe of Strichen in Aberdeenshire. Marlene was and is still well known as a teacher of Highland dancing and was approached by John Sellar of Rosehearty a few years back to introduce these type of dances when the Highland and the Country steps merged at a dance festival in Buchan. I have no doubt a lot of you have your own variations and some will disagree on the paths we have trodden on the dancefloor but these are as danced and instructed by the two ladies and that's just what I asked of them.

Last but not least is my wife Esma. How she coped with the stress of all this I'll never know—me not believing what Marlene and Margaret had written down for me and then us up on the carpet floor with a one-two-three and a one-two-three. Ach, they were right all the time!

Contents

Preface   ix
Background to the Dancing   1
A Life of Music and Dancing   11
The Basic Steps   20

THE DANCES
The Grand March   29
The Circassian Circle   31
The Friendly Waltz   33
The Dashing White Sergeant   35
The Boston Two-Step   37
The Virginia Reel   39
The Highland Schottische   41
The Four-Hand Star   43
The Pride of Erin Waltz   45
The Eightsome Reel   47
The Call o' the Pipes   50
The Mississippi Dip   52
The Eva Three-Step   54
The Lomond Waltz   56
The Lancers   58
The St Bernard's Waltz   62
The Britannia Two-Step   64
The Swedish Masquerade   66
The Gay Gordons   68
The Broun's Reel   70

THE MUSIC   73

Preface

Tootle-tootle gaed the flute, fiddle-diddle gaed the fiddle
They gaed reelin oot and in again and up and doon the middle
George Bruce Thomson
The Wedding o' McGinnis

There are many facets in the art of tripping the light fantastic in this wonderful country of ours—Highland dancing as exhibited at the Gatherings, Country dancing as portrayed by the Royal Scottish Country Dance Societies and like bodies, Old-Time Dancing and Sequence à la Victor Sylvester and the inevitable discos. There's also the devil-may-care approach often inspired by the barley bree.

A wee drappie o't, a wee drappie o't
We'll be happy a' thegither ower a wee drappie o't!

Stop! That's it! Let's have a ceilidh—why not? 'Ach bit I canna dance' is often the plaintive cry. Yes, I can sympathise with those who crouch into the corner of a hall at a wedding or similar function 'feart' that they may be dragged up on to the floor as a prize exhibit showing to all the thrawn efforts of two left feet. There is also a common fallacy that ceilidhs and Old-Time dancing requires the kilts and the ladies' dresses bedecked with tartan. Not so! Oh yes, I am proud to wear the kilt and so are others on the dancefloor but for such a dance these days it is often trousers and shirt-sleeve order for the men. No less dainty to watch and certainly no less enjoyable to execute.

But really, dancing is great fun and as at the wedding of McGinnis they certainly danced with gay abandon, which is the angle I'll be pursuing as we dance the happy hours away thumbing through the contents of this book. We're here to enjoy the experience.

It's certainly true that in large numbers all over Scotland halls have witnessed a great revival of what some term Old-Time dancing. Indeed in the radio programmes I have the privilege to present on BBC Radio Scotland I am constantly being asked for dance instructions and this book is an attempt to answer an obvious need. The Royal Scottish Country Dance Society are to be congratulated on their work as far as that area of set dances is concerned. Since their founding in 1923 they have made more and more folks aware of the enjoyment of Country dancing and now keep in touch with some 30,000 members via branches all over the world from Tokyo to Toronto and from Australia to Alberta.

The purpose of this book is also to cater for those who are interested in more general dancing and to demonstrate that you don't have to be a champion dancer to dance. After all the roads are full of motor cars and we're nae a' Grand Prix winners!

The dances chosen are all popular at venues throughout Scotland and I have deliberately omitted the foxtrots, sambas, etcetera—let's not complicate the issue—we've enough to be going on with here! The dance scene in Scotland is in a vibrant state and more and more folks are returning to the dancefloors. Jimmy Shand Jnr has for years kept Old-Time dancing to the forefront at Letham Village Hall, with dances every two weeks. From the 1950s and the dances in the Highlanders' Institute, dancers in the Glasgow area now throng to ceilidh dancing at the Riverside Club and the Renfrew Ferry.

Keep studying the local papers and listen to local radio stations as well as BBC Radio Scotland, where a spot is reserved in 'Shepherd's Fancy' for news of such events. Aye, there's room for you all on the dancefloors of Scotland. On with the ceilidh!

Robbie Shepherd

Background To The Dancing

Come screw your pins and gie's a screed
Fae your unrivalled fiddle
Nae fabled wizards wand I trow
Had e'er the magic airt o' Gow
When wi' a wave he draws his bow
Across his wondrous fiddle

Robert Burns
To Mr Gow visiting Dumfries

Our national bard's tribute to Dunkeld's Niel Gow (1727–1807). Every day someone somewhere will pick up the fiddle, the accordion or sit down by the piano and play a tune from the Gow family collections and even Niel by his own standards would surely have been amazed that his works have stood the test of time just as those of Burns. Even in the mid-1700s Niel could command a fee of some fifteen shillings for a society ball when the norm would be a third of that. There can be no doubt that the Gow family were a major influence on our dancing and music. Just look up the Royal Scottish Country Dance Society's publications to find the music acknowledged with such as 'Introduced by Nathaniel Gow in his Annual Ball in Edinburgh 1820'.

Of course Country dancing in set form had been in vogue before the 18th century. Some say it came from contrapassi, a sort of figure dance devised by Italian dancing masters. Others say it came from contre danse, meaning to dance opposite each other; but there can be little doubt that the influx of the set dances (with variations to provide new dances complimentary to the established few) took place in mansion halls up and down the country in the 1700s.

Dancing did not aye enjoy the popularity and social status it does today. The Church of Scotland in the

1

mid-17th century frowned on the so-called 'promiscuous dancing'—the thought of it—men dancing with ladies! The General Assembly passed an act prohibiting this 'evil' practice in 1649 and again in 1701 so that dancing, at least publicly, was never seen. Methinks the hoochs and reels were in full swing in the houses though, behind closed doors.

Edinburgh seems to have been the main centre of the revolution when the dancers came out of the closet and strange to say it was the upper classes who dared break the kirk's laws. In spite of the bible-thumping sermons, the dance scene became a must with the gentry, and musicians were hired to provide new tunes to suit the incoming dances. A popular dance tune at that time also today is the reel 'Deil Stick Da Minister'. One in the eye with the fiddle bow for the poor old padre!

The Edinburgh Assembly, a private association, was formed in 1723 and the purpose was to have musical evenings for the gentry; the object though, was to raise money for the poor. The dances naturally were danced to the traditional folk-style fiddle music of Scotland, and from the basic reels other forms of country dance were gradually, indeed rapidly introduced from England and the Continent.

This is why dances from the Royal Scottish Country Dance Society publications show different patterns and formations as well as different styles. For example, in our chosen programme we have The Eightsome Reel with eight dancers in a circle and then The Broun's Reel with the couples facing each other in a straight line. The Quadrilles and Lancers show most definitely the Continental influence. It always amazes me how the dancers of today can remember the pattern and the steps, with new dances continually being devised as in the 18th century for specific occasions or personalities.

Niel Gow for one provided tunes at the request of his patrons the Dukes of Atholl, and for special guests, anniversaries and other occasions. This had a trickle-down effect as servants in the 'Upstairs Downstairs' mould watched in amazement and delight and then tried out the odd reel and jig in the kitchen. I like to think that this has resulted in the different forms of, say, The Eightsome Reel, with the sedate form seen in the banqueting hall in perfect unison with the music contrasting with the 'devil-may-care' version seen in the village halls, where any pretence of following the music is often abandoned—'Ach let's hae an extra birl and get ye aff yer feet.'

> Warlocks and witches in a dance
> Nae cotillion brent new frae France
> But hornpipes, jigs, strathspeys and reels
> Pit life and mettle in their heels

Burns again—he liked his dance and his lady partners did Robbie and went to dancing lessons at Tarbolton. A perfect gentleman. The reels are still danced with the same gay abandon, the same driving music and in many cases, the same inner glow! But the cotillion was the start of the changes and many more influences from other countries have increased the variety of our social dances. Take our programme—Mississippi Dip? Pride of Erin Waltz? Swedish Masquerade? Aye, the dance scene has changed since Robbie had the witches and warlocks up dancing whilst Auld Nick screwed his pipes tae gaur them skirl and the jolly beggars danced to the fiddle.

Burns and Gow were contemporaries and there can be no doubt that the Gow family were a major influence on our social dance and music. Niel (always spelled with 'i' before 'e') was the son of a weaver and was virtually self-taught, apart from a few lessons on the violin from a John Cameron. At dances he was ably assisted by his brother Donald on cello. Among his compositions were 'Niel Gow's Farewell to Whisky', a slow air with reference to a poor harvest one year and subsequently not enough grain to supply the distilling industry. I don't imagine he was teetotal since the following year he wrote, 'Whisky Back Again'.

He had four sons of which Nathaniel, the youngest, was undoubtedly the best musician and most prolific composer of the family. One of his airs is 'Caller Herrin' , suggested, we are told, by the cries of the Newhaven fishwives blending in with the chiming of the nearby church bells, although it was Lady Nairne who penned the words we are all familiar with today.

The main period of change after the arrival of the set dances was during the advent of the polkas, barn dances and two-steps just as recently as the turn of the century, in fact well within the last two or three generations. The waltz, though, come into vogue at the beginning of the 19th century in England but took its time to get established in Scotland.

Of course the reel was the forerunner of them all and perhaps the only dance apart from the Strathspey that we can call our own. Wedding dances in the late 1800s in small crofting communities consisted mainly of reels and polkas with the odd Highland Schottische but aye the emphasis on the reel, which of course retains its popularity today. You'll find there's scarcely an end to a ceilidh without an encore after the last dance. You know what I mean—the musicians are tired, having just played the last waltz and are thinking of home and a cosy bed when the dancers, some inspired by the barley bree, converge on the floor yet again with a hooch and a skirl to summon the music for a final 'furl roon the fleer'.

It was in the aftermath of the First World War that jazz was to have a dramatic effect, with our reels and schottisches under threat. The foxtrot and the quickstep were becoming all the rage and these dances are still a feature of Old-Time dances and ceilidhs. The end of the Second World War marked a decline in ballroom dancing and for the next twenty years there was further erosion as hotel lounge entertainment and beat bands took over.

Thankfully that decline has been halted and in truth in some parts of the country, notably the West Highlands and the Borders, the interest never waned.

The start of the era of which we speak was in the late 1880s, and saw the rise in popularity of the professional dance masters, styled 'Dancie' followed by their surname. These itinerant teachers travelled on foot, then on bicycle right up till the 1940s and 50s, when they had the comfort of the motor car. They were, of course, skilled musicians too—no gramophone to assist them! They invariably played the fiddle and would teach steps, dancing as they played. Such a dancing master was Dancie Reid of Newtyle who would easily cycle ten to twenty miles a day to and from his classes scattered around his area of Angus. These teachers tended to be very strict too, with the emphasis on good manners and decorum.

The Strathspey King, James Scott Skinner of Banchory (1843–1927) was for a time a professional dance master before he achieved international fame as a fiddle player. He stopped teaching in 1885 and he was one who thought nothing of hitting a pupil over the head with his fiddle bow when he lost either their attention or his patience!

Pupils were taught Highland dancing as well as ballroom dancing with deportment and etiquette the main consideration especially for the men. For the 'country loon o' roch disposition' there was no suggestion of being termed 'cissy' as he tried to learn the intricate steps. The end product was important: 'An eye for the bonnie lassie opposite!' It was also a question of dress—gloves, patent leather shoes and the obligatory 'May I have the pleasure, please', then escorting the lady back to her seat after the dance. The girls were taught to curtsy and the men and boys to bow. It appears the teacher wasn't too fussy about attaining a high standard of technique and polish as long as the pupils got the rudiments of the figures of the dances and the correct steps. That's the aim of this book too, without the rap over the head with the fiddle bow!

It was the custom for ladies to carry small books of dance instructions in their handbags and I quote from Allan's Ballroom Guide, written in the 19th century:

> What place is so proper as the Ballroom to see the fashions and manners of the times, to study men and character, to be accustomed to receive flattery without regarding it, to learn good breeding and politeness without affectation, to see grace without wontonness, gaiety without riot, air and dignity without haughtiness and freedom without levity.

What an introduction to a wee booklet of instructions as to how to dance about eighty dances! Ah well, we would not phrase our comments that way today but there is no doubt that there is a certain aura of style and enjoyment that goes half-way towards agreeing with Mr Allan.

Needless to say, the history of such a lively tradition has its share of myth and legend. Some will tell you that the natural gesture of the male dancer in raising his arms outstretched with the fingers neatly arranged is to symbolise a stag at his courting: the king of the Scottish mountains with antlers aloft and his heart filled with pride. But perhaps we have lost a wee bit of tradition since then because in the exuberance of the ceilidh, some ladies are wont to try the same posture!

The origins of specific tunes and dances are also interesting. It is suggested that when Bonnie Prince Charlie landed in Moidart in 1745 from crossing the Sound of Arisaig from Borrodale, eight local lads working at the peats, with prior warning of his arrival, got up and danced a reel of welcome. That inspired the tune the 'Eight Men of Moidart' and the dance of the same name. Some historians will dispute this along with other aspects of Prince Charlie's adventures, but then this latter thought is dismissed by us as it doesn't inspire the dance! And when the minister was late one stormy Sunday morning at the tiny church of Tulloch many years ago, the congregation, frozen to the marrow, got up and danced a reel in the aisle to keep warm. That was the basis for the Highland dance, The Reel of Tulloch.

Country dances as distinct from Highland reels came from England in the early part of the 18th century and gradually new Scottish dances, with variations on the original, evolved to fit in with the native reels, that is, the Strathspeys, jigs and hornpipes. Other types of dance were also introduced from the Continent, with the earliest square dances coming from Paris in the 1800s after the Napoleonic Wars. Waltzes too arrived from across the North Sea, with the polka following on a few years later. The barn dance came from America around 1900 but all of these dances blossomed in England long before they caught on in Scotland.

Well, that's the dance background, so how about the music? As the song goes, you can't have one without the other and Scottish dance bands have a unique role to play. Thanks to early influences the dance bands have adopted and adapted music to suit our current varied programme as no other musical ensemble could.

In the old days, from the turn of the century up until the 1920s, the usual mix would be two fiddles and a cornet, or just a fiddle and a piano, but rarely more than a three-piece at village halls. The large centres, of course, had bigger bands, with the fiddle still predominant before the melodeon and accordion were introduced.

From the 18th century and the arrival of the set dances, we have already spoken of the influence of Niel Gow. There were others too, for example Allan Archibald, who was a player in Nathaniel Gow's band. Baptie's Musical Scotland (1894) tells us that Allan died from being maltreated by some farm servants when going home from a ball. Some musicians are never appreciated!

New compositions for the fiddle were continually being introduced and, alongside the Gows, Robert Mac-Intosh or 'Red Rob' of Tullymet must rank highly. Red Rob was born in 1745 and he was a celebrated violinist and teacher, as well as being an excellent composer of dance music, the titles of the tunes indicating the circles he moved in as musician to the society dances, for example, 'Aboyne Castle' and 'Lady Charlotte Campbells'.

William Marshall (1748–1833) also contributed a great deal. As well as being musician to the Gordon family at Fochabers, he rose to become factor of the estates of the 'Cock o' the North' the Duke of Gordon. He was certainly the best if not the first Strathspey composer of the age. The Strathspey King though, as we have mentioned, was James Scott Skinner of Banchory, and he has left an everlasting mark on our dance music—where would the elegantly-danced Strathspeys be without him?

In the 1920s, along with the fiddles and cornets, a new sound was being introduced to the Scottish dance band scene. The melodeon of the farm bothies was gaining in popularity through the records of such as the Wyper Brothers, Peter and Daniel of Hamilton.

Jimmy Shand holds a unique position in Scottish dance music and made his first record in 1933 as a soloist before forming his band. His style, his mastery of the instrument and his job as a salesmen with a music shop (Forbes of Dundee) popularised the accordion as we know it today. At the age of eighty-four he is still revered all over the world and has been honoured at the highest level as MBE, Honorary MA and Fellow of the British College of Accordionists. I once asked him to explain the unique Shand 'dunt', the immaculate timing. He replied, 'I jist watch the feet o' the best dancers in the hall.' Such modesty.

Jimmy started out his playing when he was but eight-years-old, on the humble mouth organ, a tanner moothie. (This is one area where I can rub shoulders with the maestro—where did I go wrong?) He then graduated to the Double Ray melodeon favoured by the bothy lads of the day, in farming and mining villages alike. Gradually it was to lead him (with advice and encouragement from his pals, notably Dr Sandy

Tulloch) to sound out the manufacturers and he was invited to tour the Hohner factory in Germany. This led to the unique sound of the Shand Morino and today's musicians on the accordion can vouch for his foresight in adapting the box for the Scottish idiom.

With the advent of the barn dance more pipe tunes were being adapted for the dance and Bobby MacLeod takes a great deal of credit for the introduction of the big 2/4 pipe marches from such great pipers and composers as John McColl, Willie Lawrie and George S. McLennan.

Other bands have developed over the years, with Ian Powrie and his band an influence on a lot of our leaders today. There are far too many for me to mention here and I don't want to commit myself anyway, as the impartial presenter of BBC's 'Take the Floor'! From round about four or five bands broadcasting regularly in the 1940s, nowadays it is difficult to fit any band in more than once a year and they are all of the highest standard.

Some claim now that the accordion predominates, and that it's difficult to hear the fiddle above the strength of the box. But from the days of Tim Wright and the Cavendish Band there continues to be a place for the big fiddle sounds, though costs have meant that in most cases a band rarely has more than five members at ceilidhs and Old-Time dances.

Another refreshing sound alongside the traditional set-up can be heard these days from within what might be termed the folk scene. (I dislike the differentiation though it certainly existed in my early days of attending folk sessions.) Different instrumentation is being introduced—some successful, some not—and I do applaud the use of a 'caller'. This suggests something like the barn dances in America, but specially aimed at the type of programme I portray here: you're new at the ceilidh, the band play and will you or will you not get up to dance? Any worthwhile caller will dispel doubts and give everyone the confidence 'tae get tore in'.

Another most encouraging sign is that our youthful band leaders (of which there are many) take the trouble, nay the delight, in dancing too, which brings us back to Jimmy Shand's maxim of watching the feet of the best dancers in the hall. If you can't beat them, join them and, oh yes, I have seen Jimmy up on the dancefloor too, a sedate waltz with Anne as I recall! Yes, of course the ceilidh has altered considerably, from the turn of the century. The basic ingredients though, the sheer enjoyment and the great atmosphere are still there. Thanks to the musicians and dancers alike, it's set fair for years to come—the Scottish feel for the steps, integrated with the beat of the Highland pulse will ensure that.

A Life of Music and Dancing

He blew them rants sae lively, scottisches, reels and jigs
The foalie flang his muckle legs and capered ower the rigs . . .
The feet o' ilka man and beast got yokie when he played
Hae he iver heard o' whistle like the wee herd made

Charles Murray
The Whistle

The sheer joy of making music and the exhilaration of those who are spellbound into the dance—that's the ceilidh no matter who supplies the ingredients. The wee herd was happy with his music and his instrument, however primitive, totally oblivious to the education process he was supposed to follow at school, as those who know the poem will testify. He had the whole farm household dancing and happy with it!

I couldn't emulate the young fellow as described by Charles Murray but I certainly kent how to make a whistle at his age, thanks to the finest Do-It-Yourself expert I ever knew: my late dad, Harry The Souter. Just pick a young sapling from a Rodden (Rowan) tree—'Trim it and wet it and thump it on your knee'.' Make sure it's of virgin growth with no knots in between. Keep it wet and pliable and the whole sheath—the young bark—will slip off. With a sharp knife, shave say an eighth of an inch right along the top to enable the air to get through, then carve out a larger mouthpiece at one end. Slip the bark back on and cut out the windhole notch for the music and, say, three smaller holes along the bark and wood and there's the whistle from the muckle sappy sooker. Three holes were all I could manage. You had to be a Stradivari to complete the octave! I never could.

Aye, that was about the time when an interest in Scottish dance music began to permeate the brain of this Dunecht loon. Well, the start of my abiding interest in the overall culture and the 'Spik o' the North-East'.

There was always music in our family home at Dunecht in Aberdeenshire. My mother, Nellie, played the piano in a wee dance band in the 1920s and 30s, the trio of Alex Dow's dance band consisting of fiddle, cornet and piano. She also had pupils for lessons on the piano, but—regrets!—it was lost on me then. Getting your own mother to teach you finger exercises ad nauseam from Smallwood's piano tutor was not my idea of how to spend my leisure hours, while a football was being kicked about the park in my absence.

Mum recalls with pleasure the dances she played for in the barn loft at Castle Fraser (a stately building now in the hands of the National Trust), the harvest homes with the clyack sheaf in pride of place in the barn of Waterton Farm, as well as the social occasions organised by the employees of Lord Cowdray in Dunecht Hall.

My uncles on my mother's side, Percy and Bob, went to dancing lessons in their younger days in Newmachar, suitably attired in patent shoes and white gloves and, although just ordinary apprentice tradesmen, they thought nothing of the 'dandy' look about them—'Naething cissy aboot that.' Oh me! If only they could have a look in at some of today's discos.

In telling me of her brothers, mum, at the same time couldn't recall my dad getting lessons but I do recall how he loved to dance in his own natural way and was invariably first on to the floor. I've seen a wee printed programme of the Dunecht Agricultural Club's annual dance in Dunecht Hall in 1949 and you were actually invited to search out partners from the start for a particular dance and get the favoured lady to initial it. I'll bet dad had it a' worked out well before The Grand March was underway!

My father played not a note of music but his dancing feet and overall effort would have brought praise from Victor Sylvester himself. Not that the garb on the dancefloor would have pleased the carnation-bedecked old Vic. I see him yet with the jacket off and draped round the back of some chair—Dad that is, nae Vic—the white shirt-sleeves rolled up, the galluses haudin' up the breeks and away in full flight into his favourite dance, The Broun's Reel. Now that's ceilidh dancing with a capital 'c'. He was seldom off the floor from the first dance to the last and, if you want a wee confession, I'm following my father's footsteps—I'm following my dear old dad. Well, I'm happier on the dancefloor than I was with my legs dangling in short breeks trying the scales on the family piano.

In common with most young lads and lasses, I did attend dancing classes in the early 1950s. Our tutor was Bert 'Bapper' Ewen of Inverurie—so-called because he was a baker to trade and bap is our Doric word for a bun. Bert was certainly the last of the itinerant dance masters of our area but thank goodness others have now taken up the cudgels on a voluntary basis in districts all over the country to keep the dancing alive.

We used to think it strange that this strong-looking man could be so light of foot with his dancing pumps on and he was always accompanied by his vivacious wife, Hilda, as dancing partner. Bert also ran dances on a professional basis and was an innovator too at the time in country halls. 'Jist rinning dances for his ain pooch' was the ignorant call from some folks who resented the intrusion into their territory. Understandable at the time, I suppose, since these same folks were putting all the hard work into dances for the rurals, the whist club, the flower show and such. His main base was the Railway Hall in Inverurie and he was responsible for bringing the best of our Scottish dance bands to the area, aye, and Irish groups too, with the celebrated Paddy McGarr and the Gallowglass Ceili Band the most frequent visitors.

The dancing classes I attended were held in Dunecht Hall prior to my being called up for National Service. It was a beautiful hall built by Lady Cowdray for the benefit of the tenants and workers on the estate. In the early stages of tuition, indeed at all times even at dances, all the boys would sit on one side of the hall and the girls in a row on the other, like the banks of a river and ye daurna cross the divide until told! Bert and Hilda would demonstrate to the strains of a Victor Sylvester or Jim Cameron record, depending on the chosen dance, then he would pair off the partners when some degree of proficiency had been reached by the learners.

Invariably in the tender years of youth as we surveyed the talent opposite, us lads would eye up the belle of the ball and leave the wallflowers to wither. Helen was the young stunner and there she was across the hall on the day that Mr Ewen allowed us to choose our own partner, testing out the system of decorum as laid down in Dancie Reid's days. No sooner had he switched on the gramophone, placed the needle in position and started the music with a 'Gentlemen, please take your partners for the quickstep', than we all moved en masse like a pack of hounds after the fox. Yes, the lovely Helen was our choice. In the resulting rugby scrum one lad emerged triumphant and a few of us were left lying in a heap on the floor.

My interest in music and dance was encouraged by my family's appetite for the wireless. As a boy on a Saturday evening I would be sent down to the local shop at the foot of the village for the Evening Express 'Green Final' to see how my favourite football team, the Dons, had fared that day, and then across to the garage to collect the 'weet' battery for the wireless. I was fascinated by the lines of batteries all linked together by short wires like soldiers on parade and all bubbling away as they were being recharged. Home I went to listen to the Scottish Home Service and an evening with the McFlannels and Scottish dance music.

Since then band leaders have told me that after a live broadcast they would dash off to a pre-booked dance hall within a close radius and thus make their

journey worthwhile. I recall one such occasion when
Jim Cameron's was the band on air and Dunecht Hall
was the chosen venue. They played to an over—capacity
crowd that night which I heard but could not see. I wasn't
allowed to go but since our house was only a matter of
yards away from the hall, and the windows were 'wide
tae the wa', I stood outside in the cool of the summer's
evening enthralled as Dod Ogilvie on cornet sounded
right round the village—magic! Little did I know then
that I was to become part of this wireless scene.

My dad was a Jim Cameron fan and usually once a
month he would take the bus to Aberdeen while my
brother, sister and me would eagerly await his return
with a brand new 78 record. Was it to be Cameron,
Shand or Rennie? Oh, the joys from the days of the
wind-up gramophone!

A little later in my teens, just before my stint with the
Royal Air Force and then again after I was demobbed,
I used to cycle and then motorcycle on Saturday nights
to the neighbouring village of Garlogie (some five miles
away), first to the local pub, 'Mother Allan's', and then
on to the dance in Garlogie Hall.

It was from the wee lounge of the Garlogie Bar that
I started on my musical and semi-professional stage
career. A dear old lady by the name of Mrs Baird,
came to help the Allan family after the father died.
She had been a publican herself at Balmedie and she
would come through to the lounge, sit down at the
piano and encourage us young men to have a sing-song
and a tune. That led to the formation of the Garlogie
Four, a most unlikely combination of two mouth organs,
fiddle and piano. I was the vocalist and second mouth
organ player—second moothie since I couldn't attain the
proper co-ordination on any lively set of reels and thus it
was claimed I only played every second note!

We did rather well with the group (Ronnie, Donald,
Esma and me) and appeared regularly in the 50s in the
Tivoli Theatre, Aberdeen. I remember well an article in

the People's Journal of January 1962 with the heading 'Four who met in a bar are hit on stage'. Since Esma had become my wife by then, you would have been forgiven if you had assumed we met as we slurped over a pint of beer at the bar counter. But there were no pints for ladies in those days! No, we met through my love of dancing and jigging and Esma's talent as a piano player with Adam Johnstone's Accordion Band. Esma is the musician in the family without a doubt and a fine accompanist in demand for solo players.

The Garlogie Four played for twelve years every Sunday for ceilidhs in the Douglas Arms Hotel, Banchory, and many a great night we had too. We enjoyed the music and the dancers responded. We were also the resident band for weddings at the hotel and I think our first fee was thirty shillings for the night—we weren't exactly playing for money but by jings, we enjoyed ourselves.

The more I reminisce the more it becomes obvious that music and dance have always played a major part in my life. Saturday mornings at the time I speak of for me and a few musical pals meant a chin-wag in the Volunteer Arms in Queen Street, Aberdeen—sadly knocked down to make way for redevelopment—and then up the street a few doors to Mrs Jolly's Music Shop. She was a marvellous old lady and aye had the latest music and records from the Scottish dance music scene. Much to discuss in both ports of call including the latest bands to broadcast and the cracking new tunes being introduced.

I find it strange looking back now that I was never one for the big bands and the dances in the city. I suspect the cost and the lack of transport had something to do with it but I prefer to think it's because I loved the country village hall dances. Still, I may well have missed out on something. The Tim Wright band were regular broadcasters from the 1930s to the 1950s and the band's main base was at the New Cavendish Ballroom at Tollcross in Edinburgh. The orchestration and the precision in their music made them firm favourites for the Hunt Ball and the Highland Balls from London to Skye.

And enjoyment there was a-plenty in other major centres. Aberdeen had the Beach Ballroom which in its heyday in the 1950s and 60s catered for ballroom dancing to a dedicated crowd with a resident band and regular appearances by the big bands from down south, bands such as Ted Heath or Harry Gold and his Pieces of Eight. This must have had an effect on the type of dancing being executed but the Beach also saw fit to bring Jimmy Shand north and he drew one of the biggest crowds (not to mention queues) on his first date there—1,200 folk inside and not a ticket to be had for weeks beforehand. It was maestro Shand too, in 1956 at an open air dance in Union Terrace Gardens, Aberdeen, who drew an audience of 15,000 and stopped all the traffic in the city centre. I should know because I was there watching, totally enthralled!

Jimmy was mad keen on motorbikes in his younger days and stories are legion of his driving to gigs with the members of his band. I'll leave that to others to tell but I do like the story of another band leader—I'll spare his blushes by not naming him—who transported the band in a converted ambulance. He did not disguise too much the original use of the vehicle and this enabled him to get priority booking on the ferry over the River Forth before the road bridge was built. That was until the police checked one night and found the band members in the back of the so-called ambulance having a quiet game of cards! Aye, there's laughs galore on the road as well as at the ceilidh and so it has to be to keep a contented group.

Charlie Glass, a friend and BBC colleague when he worked at Beechgrove, Aberdeen, as a commissionaire, often recalled to me his days as a ballroom attendant at the Beach, this just after the end of the Second World

War. His job, apart from spells at the door and other odd tasks, included patrol duty in the name of good taste. His patch was round the huge fountain in the middle of the floor and, on his own initiative or at the wink of the manager, he would butt in on a couple with an 'Excuse me, please don't hold your partner in that intimate way!' Aberdeen still has the Beach Ballroom and Graham Geddes and his band regularly draw in the customers, mainly for the type of dances we are to feature at our ceilidh.

Another popular dance venue in Aberdeen was the Palais de Danse and employed there as a page boy from 1928 to 1929 was Bert Murray, who was one of my musical friends from the Garlogie Hall dancing days. Bert and the members of Bill Slessor's band would pop in past the Garlogie Bar lounge on their way to the dance. Bert used to delight in telling of his days at the Palais. His role as a page boy was to escort the couples to their seats as they arrived. There were plush settees, deep carpets all round the dancefloor and the dancers themselves suitably attired to match the surroundings. At that time, Al Leslie conducted the dance orchestra and professional teachers taught the page boys to dance the Charleston and the Black Bottom so that they, the young 'uns, could demonstrate when no variety act had been booked!

But, as I said, this scene even in later years was not for me. I was at home in the village halls with a five-piece band providing that necessary Scottish flavour, the kind of dances where the attendant would take the hip flask or half bottle off you as you went in and mightily relieved you were when it was handed back to you as you went out. Most civilised dancing indeed! Now that's enough reminiscing—let's get more up-to-date.

I have been broadcasting as presenter of various programmes for BBC Radio Scotland for sixteen years and for the last eleven years have had the privilege to present the longest-running music programme in

Scotland, 'Take the Floor', which in its earlier days was simply Scottish dance music on the Scottish Home Service. It means that I don't get the same chance to take the floor myself but I assure you the enjoyment of the music and the fellowship of the folks that surround it keeps my enthusiasm as high as it ever was.

There cannot be a more friendly group of people than those who make and dance to our music. In all my years of working with the dance band musicians I can honestly say it is rare to come across jealousy or rancour. Styles may change but the underlying theme is the tradition and the obvious enjoyment in making music. Young and old combine and encouragement is meted out with sincerity.

I must mention too the importance of the experienced band leaders in handing down their skills to young musicians. Bill Black of Stanley is an outstanding example and he introduces youngsters into his band whenever an occasion arises. The late Alex MacArthur of Biggar is another that comes to mind in this respect and one of my favourite memories is of seeing the dapper Dundonian veteran fiddler Angus Fitchett, then in his seventies, sitting on the stage of the Burnett Arms Hotel in Banchory surrounded by young fiddlers, some not even in their teens, with legs dangling hardly reaching the floor, gathered for a final 'stramash' at the end of the evening and having a rare old tune together. Angus, who is small in stature himself, set himself down beside them and the smile, the obvious enjoyment as he sat there and played, said it all—nothing can separate the musician and the love of music.

> Let's have a ceilidh, come with me
> Dance to the music, merry merry music

The Basic Steps

Step we gaily on we go
Heel for heel and toe for toe

Lewis Bridal Song

Whatever you try in life, how often are you told to put your best foot forward? That applies to the enjoyment of dancing. Don't clutter up the brain with the theory of the lefts, rights and centres. Yes, I know that pretty patterns enhance the scenario and I must admit that I like to make a better job the more I repeat the basic steps of any dance—a show-off, that's me! However, I've devoted this chapter to the basics, and practice makes perfect.

SKIP CHANGE OF STEP or **TRAVELLING STEP**
(used for a reel or jig)
Fig 1 Skip forward on the left foot taking the right foot forward slightly off the ground, moving also forward.
Fig 2 Step on the right foot closing the instep of the left foot to the heel of the right foot.
Fig 3 Step forward on the right foot.

Repeat skipping forward on the right foot but if that's too complicated, walk it through and stare at your partner's actions, assuming they know better!

Right   Left
Fig I

Right   Left
Fig 2

Right   Left
Fig 3

SLIP STEP

(used in circles and danced in reel or jig time)

Fig 1 Step to the side on the ball of the left foot with the heel well off the floor.

Fig 2 Close the heel of the right foot to the heel of the left foot.

And step we gaily, on we go again!

SLIP STEP

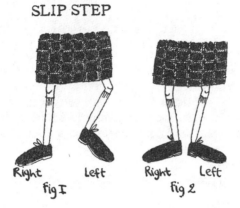

PAS BE BASQUE

Now why don't we invent our own definition? It's a long PAS (step) from the Basque country, though a similar step (The Rant Step) is attributed to Northumberland. We have danced blissfully over the years to pas de basque, one of the most common steps in Highland or ballroom dancing—A'body can paddybaa as we call it even on the disco floor.

Fig 1 Step to the side with right foot.

Fig 2 Close heel of left foot to instep of right foot taking the weight momentarily on it and lightly beat the ball of the right foot.

Fig 3 Quickly extend the left foot to the side.

It's over in a flash but how important this rhythm is. It's sheer delight as you master the technique with both feet that inch above the floor.

PAS DE BASQUE

Right Left Right Left Right Left Right Left
 Fig I   Fig 2a   Fig 2b   Fig 3

THE SCHOTTISCHE STEP

You can either face your partner with just both hands joined or you can be locked together in a waltz hold.

This is the gentlemen's step: ladies on opposite foot.

Fig 1 Hop on right foot stretching left foot to the side.

Fig 2 Hop again on right foot taking the left foot to the back of the right leg.

Fig 3 Repeat Fig 1.

Fig 4 Hop on right foot taking left foot to the front of the right leg.

Fig 5 Step left foot to side

Fig 6 Close right foot to back of left foot

Fig 7 Step left foot to side and hop.

Repeat the exercise with the left foot.

Right (HOP) Left Right Left Right (HOP) Left Right Left
 Fig I   Fig 2   Fig 3   Fig 4

Right Left Right Left Right   Left
 Fig 5   Fig 6 Fig 7

MOVEMENTS or FORMATIONS

RIGHTS AND LEFTS

(used for such as The Circassian Circle)

Fig 1 Lady stands on partner's right-hand side with both facing the couple opposite.

Fig 2 Give the right hand to the person opposite and change places.

Fig 3 Face your partner on the opposite side, give the left hand this time and change places.

Fig 4 Face the person opposite, give the right hand and change places.

Fig 5 Face partner on own side, give left hands and change places.

And you're back to where you started.

RIGHTS AND LEFTS

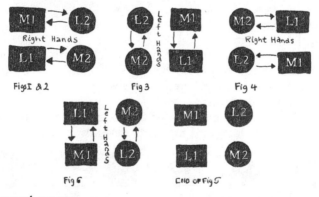

LADIES' CHAIN

Fig 1 Lady on partner's right-hand side facing the couple opposite.

Fig 2 Ladies give each other the right hands and swap places. On this movement the gentlemen dance into the ladies' place.

Fig 3 First lady turns the second man with left hand. At the same time the second lady turns the first man with left hand. Both ladies thus finish on the gentlemen's right-hand side.

Fig 4 Ladies give each other the right hands and go back to their own places.

Fig 5 Now turn your own partner with left hands to finish back in original places.

LADIES CHAIN

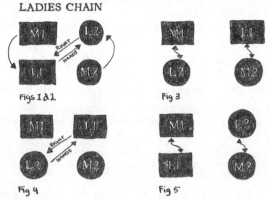

Figs 1 & 2   Fig 3

Fig 4   Fig 5

CORNERS

Fig 1 First corner

Second couple moves into first couple's place as they dance into the centre of the set. First man to face third lady, first lady to face second man.

Fig 2 Second corner

Side couples repeat as for first corners but first man faces second lady and first lady faces third man.

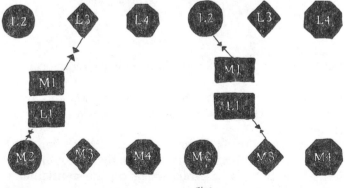

Fig 1   Fig 2

24

REEL OF THREE and **FIGURE-OF-EIGHT**
This is easy—you just weave in and out.

In Broun's Reel you start by passing first corner by the left shoulder.

In The Eightsome Reel you start by passing your partner by the left shoulder.

In The Dashing White Sergeant the person in the middle passes the person on the right by left shoulder, and then the opposite person with right shoulder.

REEL OF THREE AND FIGURE OF EIGHT

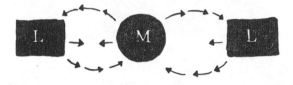

GRAND CHAIN
Just face your partners—ladies go round clockwise, gentlemen anti-clockwise. Give your right hand in passing to your partner, left hand to the next person and so on right round the circle and back to your place.

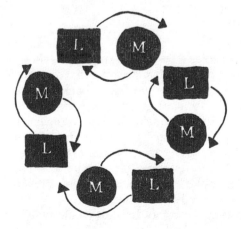

RIGHT and LEFT-HAND WHEEL
(used for The Four-Hand Star and The Lancers)

This can be danced with the lady on partner's right-hand side or with the couple facing each other.

Fig 1 Lady stands on partner's right-hand side.

Fig 2 All turn to the left. First and second ladies join right hands as do first and second gentlemen and dance four travelling steps. This is the right-hand wheel.

Fig 3 Dancers turn, join left hands and return to their places. This is the left-hand wheel.

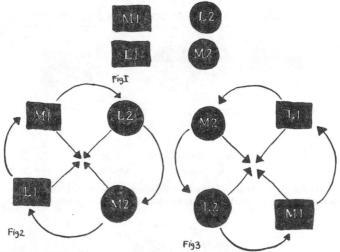

DOS-E-DOH

This is danced as a travelling step or a walk and the term comes from the French *dos à dos*, a seat on which the users sit back-to-back. Here we dance back-to-back.

Fig 1 The lady stands on partner's right-hand side facing the couple opposite. This is as for The Four-Hand Star—couples face each other for The Virginia Reel.

Fig 2 All then move towards person opposite, pass each other by the right shoulder, then move back to back round each other, pass each other by the left shoulder moving backwards into place.

No diagram—far too difficult to illustrate!

The Dances

Now the fiddler's ready let us all begin
So step it out and step it in
To the merry music of the violin
We'll dance the hours away

(as sung by the Glasgow Orpheus Choir
under Sir Hugh Roberton)

THE GRAND MARCH

The first ten dances in our programme are as described to me by Marlene Lowe so let's go to her local venue at the Ritchie Hall in Strichen where the band are all eager to get started. Right then, there is no need to be first on the floor. At a wedding reception it's usually the bride and groom who lead off, at a dance or ceilidh it would be the MC or guest of honour.

The Grand March. The 'Grand' I take to mean big and stately. It's a great opening dance for breaking the ice when there are strangers in the company. Ah! That's some up now so let's join in. I take the lady on my right arm and we march anti-clockwise round the hall. Once we've gone two or three times round and all the folks who want to dance have joined in the throng, the leading couple then march up the centre of the hall from the back towards the band with all the other couples following on behind. The couples then divide as singles with the ladies all following the first lady to the right, round the side of the floor and the gentlemen to the left.

I must admit I've done this dance often and never have I lost my partner in the middle but Marlene assures me this is how it is done in her area so who am I to argue! We always remained as couples and split alternately to the sides. Well, that's coming now as the couples meet up again at the bottom, march up the centre to the top and then do indeed split to the sides alternately with columns down both sides of the hall, first couple to the right, second couple to the left and so on.

We then meet up with the couples coming down from the opposite side and link arms as foursomes in straight lines again, marching up the middle of the hall towards the band. We split in fours and cast off as before. (Cast off? Oh sorry, I'm getting technical already—I mean we split as before.) In fours now, we go down the opposite sides of the hall and meet up linking arms as eight dancers and march to the top again.

Aye, eight folks totally relaxed, facing and acknow-
ledging the band and keeping time to the music until the
last chord is played. And that's it. Don't leave the floor
though. Let's see what the Master of Ceremonies has for
us now. With the same partner, it sometimes is a waltz
country dance or Circassian Circle with the foursomes
as arranged earlier or it could be just a couple waltz.

But just before we leave The Grand March, Marlene
tells me of another variation and here it is as a PS. The
variation comes when we reach the stage just before the
first couple come down the centre, in other words when
we are satisfied that everyone who wishes to dance is
partnered off and on the floor marching behind the first
couple. Instead of the leading couple coming down the
centre they take the dancers diagonally across the hall
towards the band's right on stage and then along the
front of the band, diagonally across the hall again to
the right-hand corner at the back and then return to the
original plan and down the centre. Got it? No? Well, it
doesn't matter, just follow the leader.

SUMMARY

1 Leading couples march with others behind until all
   eventually form a big circle around hall
2 Link arms (ladies on the right) and progress anti-
   clockwise
3 First couple lead company up towards band
4 Couples cast off alternately and progress down
   sides of hall
5 Couples link arms in fours and march up towards
   band
6 Foursomes cast off alternately and progress as in 4
7 Foursomes link arms in eights and march as in 5

Alternative

3a Couples split into singles down opposite sides of
   hall: gents go left and ladies right, meeting at the
   bottom and marching up towards band.

THE CIRCASSIAN CIRCLE

Yes, here we are still on the floor and partnered off in fours round the hall. The Circassian Circle is a progressive dance hence the need to space out to allow us to move on to other couples. The ladies are on the gents' right-hand side as before and two couples face each other.

We start off with rights and lefts which means I take the right hand of the lady opposite and change places. My partner and her opposite number do likewise. We are now all on opposite sides facing our partners. We now give left hands to our partners and change places. We are still on the opposite side but now facing the other couple again. We again join right hands and change places with them back to our own side to face each other. Once more I take the left hand of my partner, opposite couple do likewise and we should all be back to our original places. We are! That's a relief and all in time to the music too! I would need a map for revision I'm sure, but in simple terms all we have done is to make a square. It sounds complicated but it's not.

Next, I turn to face my partner and do four pas-de-basque steps (see Basic Steps) but if the mind is befuddled by this time just 'step kick' in time to the music. It won't matter as long as all the couples then swing with each other.

Now it's the ladies' chain. I and my male colleague opposite move into the ladies' places as our respective partners change with the right hand and the lady opposite turns me round with her left hand, as my partner does with her opposite. The ladies again move with the right hands and back to their original places and turn their partners with the left hands.

It does sound complicated but it's simple movements, and if you fall behind no one will mind as long as you finish up a foursome as we come to the final movement.

The Circassian Circle

I and my gentleman friend now join hands behind our partners and the ladies link on to our arms and swing round to the left in a tight little bundle, and ladies keep your feet on the floor! We break off and dance as couples in either direction to meet with another couple and the exercise is repeated all over again. Plenty of opportunity to practice!

SUMMARY   Bars

1 Sets of four, comprising two couples
2 Rights and lefts   (1-8)
3 Set and swing partner   (9–16)
4 Ladies chain   (17–24)
5 Circle and move on to next couple   (25–32)

THE FRIENDLY WALTZ

Before we get up on to the floor again, let me take you back to the comment I made of 'grand' as in Grand March. It reminds me of a tale involving the late Hector MacAndrew, that fine fiddle player from Aberdeen. Hector had been entertaining at Oldmeldrum and was invited by a well-known character to visit a relation for a tune, with the comment that the lady of the house had a 'grand' piano. When Hector arrived he was surprised to find an upright in the lounge. 'Where's the grand piano?' he enquired. Then it dawned on him that what the lad meant was that it was a grand—a very good—piano!

Ah well, back to the dancing and as a third dance this is a great way to get the dance or ceilidh in full swing. It's The Friendly Waltz. Everyone is encouraged to get on the floor—the Master of Ceremonies or the band leader will make sure of that—and again it's fine to coax the shyness out of the reluctant few left sitting in the hall.

We all form one big circle with the ladies on their partners' left. When the music starts we all join hands and swing into the centre and out again. The men then pass the ladies to their right-hand side and all join hands, swinging into the centre and out again. This time the men face their partner and the ladies curtsy. The couples now hold each other as in a waltz position and take two steps to the man's left, then two steps to the right.

Then, keeping in the circle, the couples all do a complete waltz turn and the lady finishes on her partner's right. The lady is now in position on the next gentleman's left so there's a new partner for her—and for me! Yes, each time we complete the sequence we change partners, and what could be more friendly than that?

SUMMARY   Bars

1 Couples form a big circle around hall,
   lady on gent's left
2 Join hands and swing in and out ⎫
3 Lady passes to gent's right   ⎬ (1–8)
4 Repeat 2   ⎪
5 Gentleman turns to face partner and⎪
   lady curtsies   ⎭
6 Couple take two steps to gent's left,⎫
   then two to right   ⎬
7 One complete waltz turn with partner⎪ (9–16)
   and lady finishes on the right   ⎭

THE DASHING WHITE SERGEANT

Now we come to one of the most popular set dances at any dance or ceilidh—The Dashing White Sergeant. This dance, like The Circassian Circle, can be found in the publications of the Royal Scottish Country Dance Society but the origin of the title is not Scottish. It is reputed to come from a song of the theatre of the 18th century composed by General Burgoyne. The song (with a familiar theme to it) tells of a girl who wishes to dress up as a soldier to follow her loved one to the battlefields. The dance itself belongs to the 19th century.

Now I need two partners for this one. When ladies are in short supply, one lady can be in the middle with a gentleman on either side or three of the same sex can also make up the sets—we're nae fussy. Enjoy the dance!

The set-up is similar to The Circassian Circle as we are going progressively round the room but it's six in each set. I am in the middle with a lady on either side and it's the same with the three opposite us. All six of us join hands and circle to the left for eight counts, then to the right for eight counts, finishing back at our starting places. I, being in the middle, turn to the lady on my right-hand side, dance two pas-de-basque (if you haven't mastered the intricacies of that, then swing your legs and feet in time to the music!) and then swing that lady so that I finish up facing the lady on my left. I repeat the exercise with her, finishing back between the two ladies.

We all dance a figure-of-eight (well, a reel-of-three) with our own threesomes weaving in and out, as the figure suggests, passing on the left shoulders. We then re-form as a three, joining hands, me still in the middle.

Now we advance towards the three in front of us and retire—no, not off the dancefloor!—just the obligatory advance and retire before advancing again and this time, as we are going clockwise, we form arches for the three opposite to pass under as they go in the opposite direction. Voila! There we are face to face with three more dancers and we're off again and again and again. Great fun!

SUMMARY   Bars

1 Sets of six, comprising two trios of two
   ladies and one gentleman
2 Circle to left for eight counts and
   back to the right for eight counts   (1-8)
3 Pas-de-basque two steps and gent
   swings each lady   (9–16)
4 Trios dance a figure-of-eight   (17–24)
5 Re-form then advance and retire—
   advance again, moving on to
   meet next three   (25–32)

THE BOSTON TWO-STEP

The Boston Two-Step was introduced in 1908 by Tom Walton and selected for championships no less, being made up of graceful pas-de-basque steps and balletic and theatrical dancing. No doubt when danced to perfection it is championship material but me, I like the free and easy feel to it. It is undoubtedly the most popular dance in the Shetland Islands and at their annual festival of Up Helly-A, I've seen practically every second dance as a 'Boston'.

Talking of Shetland, have you ever tried to dance aboard the Aberdeen-Lerwick ferry, the St Clair, with the gales howling and the seas gurly? I have—the accordionist strapped to a pole on the dancefloor and The Boston Two-Step not as graceful as Tom Walton would have wished. There's me and my partner stotting from one side to the other with some rather impromptu steps.

Back to the dancefloor at Strichen now and Marlene's steps for the dance. It's a couple dance of course and we're not first on the floor this time so we'll take our cue from those already dancing.

My partner is on my right-hand side, me holding her by the hand. We pas-de-basque away from each other then in towards each other. We then both walk forward four steps and turn and repeat just as we have done back the other way starting with the opposite foot. Again if the pas-de-basque is beyond you, you can just step forward on your left foot and swing your right foot forward, step back on your right foot and close your left foot. Remember though that you and your partner must do the same thing. In the latter movement, my partner would start on her right foot.

After the four steps sequence, we're back to our place. Now we face each other with both hands joined and dance two pas-de-basque (or step and swing in time to the music). Now I take two steps to my left as my partner makes a complete turn to her right. We join in a waltz hold and dance round together for four bars if you can make it, ready to start all over again, moving progressively round the hall.

In Shetland there's a part of the dance where they all momentarily form a huge circle with a couple of steps and a michty 'hooch', hands outstretched touching fingers to fingers. This makes for good ceilidhing, but here we have Marlene's dance and I would only complicate things unnecessarily if I started doing that here!

SUMMARY   Bars

1 Couple dance
2 Pas-de-basque away and together, forward four steps, turn and repeat, back to place   (1–8)
3 Face each other and pas-de-basque twice ⎫
4 Gent takes two steps to the left while lady makes complete turn to the right ⎬ (9–12)
5 Join in waltz hold and turn together   (13–16)

THE VIRGINIA REEL

Well, The Boston Two-Step can be a lively enough dance but here's a livelier one still and a dance I only attempted for the first time this year under the able guidance of Jessie Stuart at one of her dances in Dufftown. Jessie is another who has done much to stimulate interest in the Old-Time and Country dancing in her area. Then, on my next visit to Strichen, I started raving about The Virginia Reel to Marlene. I found myself promptly hauled up on to the floor and yes, I had completely forgotten how to do it.

So I listen very carefully as once more I ask Marlene to be my partner. The tunes for the dance—American folk tunes and songs—make for all the more enjoyment. 'Turkey in the Straw' is just the tonic to get you going.

The Virginia Reel is a set dance for four couples. The top of the set is nearest the band and that's where I am with my partner. The four men are standing to the right-hand side of the band in a straight line down the hall, the ladies standing opposite their partners. The music starts and we're off.

All the ladies join hands, and likewise the men. Both lines of four then advance towards each other and retire, twice. Then the four couples turn their partners right round into their place on the floor by extending right hands. The turn is repeated, this time with the left hands and then all turn their partners again, with both hands extended and held.

After that, we all dos-e-doh (see Basic Steps), really just a walk in which we pass our partners by the right shoulder. We stand facing our partners then move towards them, passing as I said by the right shoulder, then move back to back round each other passing by the left shoulder, and moving backwards into place.

Now, as first couple, where do we go from here? Well, my partner and I join right arms and swing each other down the set as far as the fourth couple. When we get there, we drop arms and I turn the fourth lady with my left arm whilst my partner turns the fourth man with her left arm. We then turn each other with our right arms and we work up the set like that. It's exactly as you would do in a Strip The Willow, assuming you know how to do that!

When we reach the top of the set again, we separate and the other three men follow me and the ladies follow my partner as we turn outwards away from each other and down the outside of the set. We meet at the bottom and lead the other three up towards the band. When they are in place, these three couples join hands making an archway under which my partner and I dance to the bottom of the set. The whole sequence is repeated until all four couples have been at the top.

It sounds complicated, I know, and this is one dance for which I do recommend you make sure that, at the top to start, you have a couple who know how to do it. After that, follow the leader and you can't go wrong!

SUMMARY   Bars

1	Sets of four couples, with ladies and gents in rows facing each other	
2	Advance and retire twice	(1–8)
3	Turn with the right hand ⎫	(9–16)
4	Turn with left hand ⎭	
5	Turn with both hands ⎫	(17–24)
6	Dos-e-doh ⎭	
7	Swing to bottom of the set	(25–32)
8	First couple turns other couples with left arms and their own partner with right arm	(33–48)
9	Men follow first man (ladies first lady) out and down side of set; meet at bottom and lead up to top	(49–56)
10	First couple come down set under arch made by the three other couples' arms	(57–64)
11	Repeat with new couple at top until all couples have been through	

THE HIGHLAND SCHOTTISCHE

The Highland Schottische was introduced in 1855 and was known by the name of the Balmoral Schottische. Now here's a dance with a real Scottish feel to it but, according to Marlene, it's one of the most difficult to describe—so where does that leave me? Yes, I've danced it thousands of times, but whether I knew my lefts from my rights is debatable.

Up on the floor again with my partner and this time we start as in a waltz hold. This one needs perfect co-ordination between partners and whatever I describe as doing with my right foot my partner is complementing with the other. Lack of co-ordination will ruin the grace and the enjoyment completely, to say nothing of the discomfort of trampled corns.

Well, I've anticipated the music and with a 'hop a little on my little right shoe' I immediately point the left foot outwards. I repeat the exercise of the hop on the right foot but this time I place my left foot round the back of the calf of my right leg. I hop again on my right foot and point my left leg again in the forward position. Hop again and then place the left foot in front of the right leg.

Got it so far? Good! Remember what I do in these first movements, my partner does in complementary style on the opposite leg (see Basic Steps for the Schottische).

Now I move my left foot to the side, as in a travelling motion, and close my right foot to back of my left. We both step sideways and now I step left foot to the side again and hop on that left foot. We repeat all this sequence from the start but back the way with the different leg as leader. We then step to the side, me on my left foot, my partner on her right, close the other foot behind the leader, step to the side again with the same feet and I hop on my left foot. Repeat this wee bit in the opposite direction leading with my right foot, then we both turn together, step hop four times and, would you believe, we're ready to start again! What a complicated mass of words for such a short sequence. Ach, never mind, practice makes perfect!

SUMMARY   Bars

1 Couple dance
2 Right foot hop, left foot outwards.
   Right foot hop, left foot to back. Right
   foot hop, left foot forward and out.
   Right foot hop and left foot at front.
3 Left foot to side and close back of   (1–4)
   right foot to back of left.
   Step left and hop.
4 Repeat 2 and 3 in opposite direction
   with opposite legs
5 Step, close, step and hop to gent's
   left, then repeat to right   (5–6)
6 Both turn together and step hop
   four times   (7–8)

Who asked me to do this anyway? Hope you understood it all!

THE FOUR-HAND STAR

Our next dance is another round-the-room dance for two couples showing the same set-up and progression as in The Circassian Circle. The Four-Hand Star also has in it distinct traces of The Virginia Reel.

I line up as usual with my partner on my right-hand side and we face the couple opposite. As soon as the music starts, the men join right hands, as do the ladies, to form the spokes of a wheel—the two pairs of hands together form the 'axle' or a four-hand star, as the title suggests. We all dance around for four counts, then we all turn and join left hands and do likewise, dancing back to our original places.

Next, we tackle the ladies' chain as in The Circassian Circle. Myself and my male colleague in the quartet move into the ladies' places whilst the ladies change, giving right hands on passing. The men give left hands to the lady coming towards them and turn right round together. The ladies again give right hands, crossing as before and turning their own partner with the left hand.

Now it's 'dos-e-doh' time again. Consult the Basic Steps if you feel like it but let's talk it through now on the dancefloor. We're facing our opposite couple again of course and then we all move forward towards the person opposite, pass each other by the right shoulder, then move back to back round each other, and so to our places. Now we turn to our partners and repeat the dos-e-doh with them.

And we're ready for the next couple. I join hands with my partner, advance towards the couple in front of us (the ones we've been dancing with) and retire. We advance again and as we're going clockwise round the room, we raise our arms for the other couple to pass through and on to pastures new! Simple, but fun.

SUMMARY   Bars

1 Sets of four, comprising two couples
2 Right-hand wheel   (1–4)
3 Left-hand wheel   (5–8)
4 Ladies' chain   (9–16)
5 Dos-e-doh round person opposite
   and dos-e-doh round partner   (17–24)
6 Advance and retire   (25–28)
7 Advance again and move on to next
   couple   (29–32)

THE PRIDE OF ERIN WALTZ

Now this dance will be more familiar to most of you but then again it's maybe years since you've attempted it and I advise you to stick to the rule of waiting for the 'experts' to get on the floor first!

The dance, in spite of its name, did not originate in Ireland though there must be connections. It was devised in 1911 by Charles Wood who officiated at the Palace Ballroom in Leith at the time. I must admit it's a favourite dance of mine—there's something in it (as the title suggests) of pride and style. A graceful dance.

As usual I have my partner on my right and this time we're standing side by side, holding hands. We start walking forward, me leading with my left foot, my partner with her right. So it's left foot, right foot, left foot. Close right foot to left foot and step forward with left foot (partner using opposite feet). Now we turn and do the same back the way except this time I lead off with my right foot, my partner with her left. Now here comes the fancy bit.

We face each other and join both hands. Now I cross my left foot over my right foot and point my right foot to the side. At the same time my partner crosses her right foot over her left foot and points her left foot to the side. Now we do it the opposite way—I cross my right foot over my left foot and point my left foot to the side and my partner crosses her left foot over her right foot and points her right foot to the side.

We then make a complete turn away from each other and finish facing each other (four steps) and with both hands joined we advance to each other and retire (two steps). I keep hold of my partner's right hand and, as we change sides, my partner turns under my arm (two steps). We repeat this back to our own sides.

Now we join in the waltz hold and both take two steps to my left, then back two steps to my right, and we dance a complete waltz turn. And on the timing of the music—keep your ears attuned—we're back to square one.

SUMMARY   Bars

1 Couple dance
2 Both move forward, man with left
   foot, lady with right; turn and repeat   (1–8)
   back the way we came
3 Cross feet and point—and repeat ⎫
   with other leg   ⎬ (9–16)
4 Partners circle away from each other ⎭
   and finish facing each other
5 Advance, retire and change
   places—then repeat   (17–24)
6 Dance two steps to gent's left, two to
   the right   (25–28)
7 Complete by waltzing with partner   (29–32)

THE EIGHTSOME REEL

My, how time flies when you're having fun! This is the last dance before the interval and the last one of the ten selected by Marlene Lowe and explained to me as we dance. Thanks, Marlene—one more time—may I have the pleasure please for The Eightsome Reel? Then you can retire to the side to lick your wounds.

Now the eightsome reel used to be a favourite dance of mine in my younger days but either old age is creeping on or else there are too many variations in different parts of the country because I invariably land in a set that 'canna dee it my wye'. I prefer to think it's the latter but Marlene is the boss—let's do it her way.

We start in a square formation, eight to a set, ladies on their partners' right:

> First couple—backs to the band
> Second couple—to first couple's left side
> Third couple—opposite first couple
> Fourth couple—to first couple's right side

Part One

The eight of us in the set join hands and circle to the left for eight counts and then back to the right for eight counts, finishing in our starting places. Next is the cartwheel. We all keep hold of our partner's hand, the four ladies swing into the centre joining right hands and we dance half way round to opposite places (four steps). The men than take over by swinging into the centre still holding our partner's hand and joining left hands to dance back to our places.

We then all turn and face our partner, dance four pas-de-basque steps (still not up to that routine? Then just step or kick your legs in time to the music) and we swing our partners. We finish up facing our partners for the grand chain. This is a simple movement involving the eight of us. We start by giving our partners the right hand in passing, left hand to the next person and so on till we have weaved back into our original places.

Part Two

The first lady dances into the centre of the square and does the pas-de-basque (or again just steps in time to the music) whilst the other seven circle round and back as at the start of the dance. Then she turns and faces her partner and they both dance two pas-de-basque steps before joining both hands to dance another two pas-de-basque steps together, turning round once. She then turns and faces the third man and repeats as with her partner.

The first lady finishes back facing her own partner and, alongwith the third man, the trio dance a figure-of-eight by passing left shoulders to start. She finishes back in the centre, the other seven repeating the circle to the left and right. She then turns to the fourth man, starts as with previous first and third men, this time involving the second man as the trio. At the end of this figure-of-eight she dances back beside her own partner and the second lady replaces her in the centre. This section of the dance is repeated by the remaining ladies and then it's the turn of the men, starting with first man. I'm certainly glad of that as it has given me plenty of time to study the movements!

Part Three

When the last man has danced back to his place, we repeat part one and that's the reason for splitting the dance into parts! Well, Marlene, it's certainly not the way I used to do it but then again it does cut down the risk of being danced off your feet!

Thanks again for the dance. Time for the Interval!

SUMMARY	Bars
1 Sets of eight, comprising four couples	
2 Circle to the left, then back to the right	(1–8)
3 Ladies wheel half-round, right hands joined; men's wheel back, left hands joined	(9–16)
4 Set and swing partner	(17–24)
5 Grand chain right round	(25–40)
6 First lady in centre while others circle to the left and back	(41–48)
7 First lady sets to and turns partner, then third man, figure-of-eight	(49–64)
8 Repeat 6 and 7 with fourth and second men—first lady back to place	(65–88)
9 Each lady in turn, starting with own partner, repeats 6 and 7 & 8	(89–232)
10 Each man in turn, starting with own partner, repeats 6 and 7 & 8	(233–424)
11 Finish dance by repeating 2–5	(425–464)

THE CALL O' THE PIPES

'Swap deems an' furl.' That was a favourite expression of the late Jock Morgan, the Kemnay fiddler who enthralled his audiences on the Music Hall stage with the dexterity of his fiddle playing and the humour in his rich north-east voice. It applies to the reels of three we've described earlier and it means simply that you just change partners and reel on the set once again.

Well, swap deems and furl is exactly what I'm doing now as I leave the Ritchie Hall in Strichen at half-time and go down to the Dean Tavern in Newtongrange to be guided through my paces in the next ten dances by Margaret Smith.

Let me extend the interval a little then to get my breath back and to let you finish your half-time snack or supper, so essential to the ceilidh. A favourite dish, especially in the north-east of Scotland, is a plate of stovies (stoved potatoes) complete with oatcakes, beetroot and a glass of milk. Now dance that off and you'll have no complaints in the morning! In Shetland you may well get a plate of thick soup that has the spoon standing upright like an oil rig in the North Sea, followed by the reestit mutton, a salty diet that fair works up a thirst. At a wedding in Orkney, they pass round the bride's cog with a punch of local flavour.

But I digress. The band are on stage so it's time for my first dance with Margaret. It's one called 'The Call o' the Pipes' and what an apt title to stir the blood of the Scottish dancer.

I have Margaret on my right as is usual for a couple dance. I hold her left hand with my right and we face round the room. We both start off on our right foot, walk four steps forward and reverse four steps back. We link right arms and half-turn to opposite sides. Now we link left arms and half-turn again, back to our own places. We take up waltz position and slip one step forward, me on my left foot, feet together, slip one step back on my right and feet together again. Still in waltz position, we do three full rotary turns to finish with the bars of music.

Now there's a nice easy one to start the second half—just remember to fit in the different movements to the music.

SUMMARY   Bars

1	Couple dance	
2	Walk four steps forward and reverse four steps back	
3	Link right arms and half-turn	(1–8)
4	Link left arms and half-turn back to your place	
5	Waltz position, slip one step forward, then feet together	
6	Now slip one step back and feet together again	(9–12)
7	Three full rotary turns	(13–16)

51

THE MISSISSIPPI DIP

Well, in the first half we had The Virginia Reel and what's this now? The Mississippi Dip? I can't quite relate that to the Scotland I was brought up in, with the Music of the Spey, The Loch ⊤ay Boat Song, The Winding Forth and the Banks of the Silvery Dee.

This dance, like The Pride of Erin Waltz we had in the first half, was devised by Charles Wood in 1911 and I wonder if perhaps it was inspired by the variety shows featuring plantation songs, etcetera, from across the Atlantic which were so popular in the music halls and ballrooms at this time.

It's a fine dance but for me it requires a lot of concentration, specially after the stovies and the interval dram! It's the dip in the title that aye catches me out. Right Margaret—prop me up if I should take a dip too far!

We again take up the waltz position and I am facing the wall as are all couples, in a circle round the room. We walk four steps back to the centre, me starting on my left foot, side balance forward on the left, then side balance back. We then walk—what an ungainly term for a dance step but then again this is a ceilidh!—four steps out again towards the wall, side balance forward and side balance back. What's all this 'side balance'? Well, side balance is quite simply taking the weight on the foot forward and again on the foot back, like a hesitation before you make the next move.

With arms round each other's waist, we walk three steps forwards (as always left to lead for me, right foot for partner) and lady turns on the third step to walk three steps back—I, at this movement, walk three steps in reverse, both back to our place. We then waltz three full turns, finishing facing the line of the dance round the room. Still with arms round our waists, we drop the waltz hold and take one step, me with the left, partner with the right, and dip on opposite foot. I then take my left foot forward again (partner right) and close my feet. We repeat the process of the dip. Woah! I've made it—the dip can be tricky but one of you will support the other!

Now with arms still round each other's waist, we walk three steps forward, my partner turning on the third step to walk three steps back as I walk three steps in reverse as we danced before the dip. Finally we take up the ordinary waltz hold and dance three full turns.

That's it! Now we've dipped our toes in the Mississippi and come out unscathed!

SUMMARY   Bars

1   Couples form a big circle around hall
2   Walk four steps to centre, side balance
    forward, then side balance back   } (1–8)
3   Walk four steps out again, side balance
    forward and side balance back
4   Three steps forward; lady turns to walk
    three steps back as gent walks in   } (9–16)
    reverse
5   Waltz three full turns
6   Take one step forward and dip on
    opposite foot, step forward again and   } (17–24)
    close feet
7   Repeat dip process
8   Repeat 4
9   Waltz to finish, with three turns   } (25–32)

THE EVA THREE-STEP

Well, that's The Mississippi Dip safely negotiated. Here we are then on to the third dance under Margaret Smith's instructions at the Dean Tavern, and this time it's an Eva Three-Step.

This dance was devised in 1904 by Sydney Painter of Manchester for his daughter. Sydney weighed in at around eighteen stone but was reputed to be as light as a feather on his feet. And me only ten and a half stone—sorry Margaret, but let's dance again!

As in The Call o' the Pipes, I have my partner on my right, holding her left hand with my right and facing round the room. As ever I start on my left foot with my partner on her right. We walk three steps forward and close our feet together. We then move three steps sideways crossing over with me behind my partner. Again we close feet. It's then a case of another three steps sideways this time with me going in front of my partner and this takes us back to our original places, closing feet again of course. We now join hands again and walk three steps backwards. From there we do an outside turn away from our partner to finish facing each other.

Taking up the ordinary waltz position, we slip one step forward and close feet together, slip one step back and close feet together. We then finish off by doing three full waltz turns, assuming we've kept up with the music! And usually, when the three sideways steps are taken, both partners clap their hands on taking up opposite sides and again when returning to original places.

SUMMARY   Bars

1   Couple dance
2   Walk three steps forward and close feet ⎫
    together (woman crosses over in front   ⎪
    of the man)   ⎪
3   Walk three steps sideways and close   ⎪
    feet together, crossing over to opposite ⎪
    sides (woman behind man)   ⎬
4   Move three steps sideways again and   ⎪   (1–8)
    close feet together, moving back to   ⎪
    original places   ⎪
5   Walk three steps backwards   ⎭
6   Separate turns outwards and face   ⎫
    partner   ⎪
7   Slip one step forward and close feet   ⎬
    together   ⎪   (9–12)
8   Slip one step back and close feet   ⎭
    together
9   Rotary waltz three full turns   (13–16)

THE LOMOND WALTZ

The Lomond Waltz is a particular favourite with dancers in the Lothians and Borders and I recall it was a favourite too of the late great Mull maestro, Bobby MacLeod. As well as being a band leader and accordionist of top quality, Bobby was a piper, a Highland dance enthusiast and an expert on the dance scene.

He observed the different tempos and styles of dancing as he played all over the country. In his excellent wee book Pas-de-bas ,which he wrote in 1984 just seven years before he died, he stressed the importance of a band leader adjusting to regional differences and witnessed the comparison of the pas-de-bas of a Highland dancer to the 'flat-footed' style of the Old-Time dancers. After his music, said Bobby, the band leader's most valuable asset is to be able to pas-de-bas. Well, we don't use that step here but, as I said, this was one of Bobby's favourite dances.

We're in the normal waltz position this time and the dance begins with the couple together making a square. We start by taking two steps to my left and two steps backwards towards the centre. Then we take two steps to my right and two forward, completing the imaginary square. These walking steps, Margaret tells me, are called chasse steps—it's one, close, two, close, with the same foot, and that's it!

Now we do a half-turn back to back and a half-turn back again to face each other. Holding both hands now we balance forward and back, then change places. To do this my partner goes under my left arm. Again we balance forward and back and return to our original places.

Now I put my left foot to the side, cross my right foot over my left foot, point my left foot to side and close feet together. My partner (still in waltz position) does the same movement and puts right foot to side, crosses left foot over right foot, points right foot to side and closes feet together. We repeat this whole part again but back the way, that is, I put right foot to side, cross left foot over right, point right foot to side and close feet together, while my partner puts left foot to side, crosses right foot over left, points left foot to side and closes feet together. That sounds like we're getting our feet in knots but when you're doing it in time to the music it just falls into place. We finish off by doing three full rotary waltz turns.

SUMMARY
Bars

1	Couple dance	
2	Gent leads by stepping two to the left and two steps backwards	
3	Gent leads by stepping two to the right and two steps forward. Couple has now completed a square.	(1–8)
4	Half turn back to back, then half turn back again	
5	Balance forward and back and change places	
6	Repeat 5 to original places	(9–20)
7	Gent points left foot to side, crosses right foot over, points left foot and closes feet together. Lady same movement using opposite feet.	
8	Both repeat 7 back the way	(21–28)
9	Waltz three full turns.	(29–32)

THE LANCERS

The Lancers is a good old-fashioned dance with regional variations. For many years it was danced all over at every dance but then suddenly it faded from the scene—perhaps it was too energetic. There are, however, distinct signs of its return, as it's included at most dances held in rural areas with the younger set all eager to learn it, and all the young players desperate to get the music for it.

The most popular version is called the Student Lancers and is as follows.

The dance is made up of four couples standing in a square, the lady on the gent's right. The first couple is the couple with backs to the band, the third couple are opposite them and facing the band. The second couple is on the first man's left and the fourth couple is on the first lady's right. This must be remembered throughout the dance.

But here now I have a problem or two trying to put Margaret's instructions into black and white. Bear with me—it is a lengthy one!

First Figure
Introduction—honour your partner and your corners. Oh, I'll have to explain that. Corners are easy because the eight (as described) are in square formation, and 'honour your partners' means a bow or curtsy before we set out on our travels.

Throughout the first figure you dance your partner and your corners. The corner you dance is first lady and fourth man. Second lady and first man, third lady and second man, fourth lady and third man.

First lady and third man advance to centre of set and turn four times, finishing in their own positions. First and third lady change places across the set, then first and third men change places across the set. Ladies

58

return to their own places, then men return to theirs and forsake their partners for four rotary turns with the corner partners.

This is repeated with third lady and first gent again opposite each other, advancing to centre and dancing four rotary turns. Ladies crossing over, gents crossing over, ladies crossing back, gents crossing back and all dancing four rotary turns with their respective corners.

This part of the dance is repeated with the second lady and fourth man turning and crossing over and back as above and then fourth lady and second man taking the lead and doing likewise. That concludes the first figure. Make sure you're not the leading couple and observe!

Second Figure

Honour partners and corners. First and third couples join right hands with their partners and advance to centre. Before returning to his own place, gent passes lady to his opposite side and advances to centre of set again. First lady and third man are facing each other as are first man and third lady. They take up waltz position and waltz to the gents' places. Ladies then cross over to their own partners and rotary waltz four turns.

Repeat this all over again with the same couples, then the whole process is danced twice again, this time with second and fourth couples.

Third Figure

Honour partners and corners. All ladies advance to centre and retire. Gents advance and clasp hands with opposite men. Ladies link arms with adjoining men. All circle to the left, breaking off when reaching own place.

All men advance and retire, advance again and place left hands on opposite men's shoulders. Men then put right arms around partners' waists and cartwheel—skip—round to original places.

Repeat all that part again but this time when the men put their arms around their partners' waists, the partners face the opposite way and cartwheel or skip clockwise—that is, men are doing cartwheel backwards and ladies facing forward, round to original places.

Fourth Figure
This figure is called Visitations and also begins by honouring partner and corners.

First and third couples visit (using a waltz step) second and fourth couples respectively, that is, first and second couples meet and third and fourth couples meet.

Ladies join right hands and gents do likewise across ladies hands and dance round for four steps, change to left hands and dance back again.

First and second couples and third and fourth couples link arms and turn in their circle for four rotary turns and stop at their respective places. First and third couples repeat all that part again but this time first couple meets fourth couple and third couple meets second couple.

They repeat the whole part involving right hands across and round, left hands across and back, then link arms and turn their rotary turns.

Repeat all of that figure again, this time second and fourth couples taking the lead, that is, second couple meets third couple, fourth couple meets first couple, right hands round, left hands back, then rotary turns, then second couple meets first couple and fourth couple meets third couple. Right hands round, left hands back and rotary turns to finish.

Every couple should have visited and danced every other couple in turn—short visits indeed!

Fifth Figure
Chord only—grand chain
We start here with the grand chain, that is, right hands to your partner and ladies go to the left, gents to the right. Half-way round the circle, you meet your partner, set to each other and continue the other half of the chain until you meet your partner again.

Dance four rotary turns then take up a straight line,

ladies in front of their partners, facing the band. The order is first, second, then fourth and third couples. Ladies slip to the left side, gents to the right, then advance to centre of dance and pass right through to opposite sides.

Ladies join hands, gents join hands, all in straight lines down the dance. Both sides advance and retire and take up original places in the set and you turn once with your partner before going into the grand chain again.

This is repeated three times more, with the third couple facing away from the band in the line this time. The order being third, second, fourth and first couple in the line. Repeat the advance and retire, straight lines down the dance and so on, as above, until the grand chain again.

The third time the straight line is made it's the second couple, first couple, third couple and fourth couple. Instead of facing up and down the dance, the line is made across the dance this time, followed by advance and retire, pass through and so on, to grand chain again.

The final line is across the dance with the fourth couple, third couple, first couple, second couple in order for the line across. Repeat the advance and retire, pass through to do your final grand chain.

Usually after the last grand chain, the band plays eight extra bars when each couple does a long rotary turn in their own place, or in some areas the gents join left shoulders and take their partners round the waist and cartwheel anti-clockwise as in the third figure.

Well, we've made it but there is no way that I can summarise as in the previous dances. There are no short-cuts here, but the figures in sequence are:

First Figure—Mainly corners	(1–104) bars
Second Figure—Centres	(1–104) bars
Third Figure—Cartwheels	(1–72) bars
Fourth Figure—Visitations	(1–104) bars
Fifth Figure—Grand chain	(1–216) bars

THE ST BERNARD'S WALTZ

Exhausted? Never! I've always found with the variation of movements and dance steps in The Lancers that it has a revitalising effect on me. It's maybe just the relief of getting through the five figures.

Anyway, let's reduce the pace a wee bit and this dance surely won't take much explaining as it's one of the most popular of them all. I've never seen a St Bernard dog waltz, though they do on occasions carry the hip flask necessary for a ceilidh, and I've no idea how the dance got its name. I do know, however, that it's a lovely dance to do, so— Margaret, mind if we dance again?

Once more, it's the normal waltz hold, my partner facing the centre of the room and me facing the wall. We start off by gliding, rather than stepping, three steps to my left with my partner obviously setting off on her right foot to complement my left. Then we touch heels down on the fourth beat. That's as far as we go that way and so we glide two steps to my right.

We then take two steps (or glides) backwards, starting again on my left foot, towards the centre. We repeat this movement back to original position, that is, gent glides two steps forward while lady glides backwards.

I then slip my left foot to the side, cross my right foot over my left whilst my partner turns under my right arm. We finish by waltzing three turns, making sure that we are in position to start afresh with the music.

Margaret tells me that in many parts of the Lothians and Borders, the lady turning under the gent's arm has been replaced with the couple taking up a waltz hold all the way through the dance and after the two steps back and forward, they slip one step forward, feet together, one step back, feet together, then waltz. I must admit I often try both ways in the same dance—it makes for variety and I also confess that instead of the sedate 'heels down on fourth beat', I often stamp my feet to let them be heard around the hall. Most satisfying!

SUMMARY	Bars

1 Couple dance
2 Glide three steps to the gent's left and touch heels down (1–4)
3 Glide two steps to the gent's right ⎫
4 Gent two steps backwards ⎭ (5–8)
5 Repeat 4 in opposite direction
6 Gent slips left foot to side, crosses right foot over while lady does one turn under gent's right arm. ⎫⎬⎭ (9–12)
7 Waltz three full turns (13–16)

THE BRITANNIA TWO-STEP

This is another dance coming to us from across the border in the early part of the century and although we have included The Britannia Two-Step away down the programme, Margaret Smith tells me that if it is put on early in the evening it can be made progressive and is again a good way of mixing the company and getting the ceilidh in full swing.

This time we require three dancers. I've already asked my two ladies up but as I said earlier for The Dashing White Sergeant, depending on the ratio of ladies to gents, it can be danced as one gent and two ladies, one lady and two gents or indeed three of the same sex. We assume here it's two ladies at either side of the gent and the progressive part I'll explain after we dance it as planned.

The gent holds his partners' hands. All three dancers do a heel-and-toe beginning on their left foot—point outwards with heel on floor and toe upwards then take back the left foot with toe pointing to floor—that leads us in to slip two steps sideways. Another heel-and-toe with the right foot and we return with two steps sideways, back to our original positions. To remind you of the slip step, it's nothing more than a step to the side on the ball of the left foot with the heel well off the floor and then close the heel of the right foot to the heel of the left foot.

You will notice at this stage that all three are on the same foot, starting with the left. All three dancers now walk three steps forward and then three steps backwards, me in the middle still holding hands with my partners. I break from that now though to do a couple of pas-de-basque steps and this is the complicated bit—at least on paper but not in dance execution.

I turn and face the lady on my left and do half a pas-de-basque—left foot to the side and close heel of right foot, then in one movement I turn on that right foot and complete the pas-de-basque with the partner on my right.

I then do another pas-de-basque as both ladies turn under my arms. (Remember if you haven't mastered the step, then swing your right leg in front of your left and then your left in front of your right. . . Margaret will crucify me for this!) All three dancers walk three steps forward and three steps back, as we did at the start of the dance.

And that's it first time through—heel-and-toe and we're away again. I love this dance: it's lively, it's fun and it's a chance to enjoy the company of two ladies of my choice. Oh, on that score I must remember to keep the peace and pas-de-basque to the ladies in alternate turns, that will be the lady to my right next time.

To finish, let me explain now the progression I spoke of earlier. This is done with the gent moving forward on the last three steps forward and back but these instructions must be made clear at the start, otherwise it gets afa confusing! And if your company makes up some trios with two-thirds men and some two-thirds ladies, try not to end up like the set Margaret told me about, where a gentlemen in trousers progressed on to join two of his own kind in kilts!

SUMMARY

Bars

1	Sets of three, any combination	
2	All three dancers on left foot to start, heel-and-toe and slip two steps sideways	
3	Repeat 2 with right foot	(1–8)
4	Three steps forward and three steps back	
5	Gent pas-de-basque with ladies and a second pas-de-basque as ladies turn under his arms	(9–12)
6	All three dancers take three steps forward and three steps back	(13–16)

THE SWEDISH MASQUERADE

Now here's an unusual title for a dance at a Scottish ceilidh or Old-Time dance. Margaret tells me it's a fairly new dance (well, in our dancing circles) but the three tempos make it very interesting and great fun. As I said with The Lancers, there's nothing like variation to sharpen the brain and heighten the enjoyment.

It's a couple dance, of course, and we start facing round the room—all in the same direction—let's say anti-clockwise with my partner on my right and me holding her hand.

We walk eight steps forward, turning on the eighth step and changing hands as we turn. Walk the eight steps back, again turning on the eighth step and changing hands back to our original positions.

The music then changes, breaking into a waltz and we continue without a pause. Still holding hands, we do a pas-de-basque twice. We then take up the waltz position and do two full rotary turns.

We then repeat everything from the pas-de-basque to the rotary turns.

As the music is entering into the third tempo, there is no time to waste and, happily, no further instructions necessary. As the reel follows the waltz, we just move up a gear and repeat as we did on that waltz section, dancing it through twice also.

Now we're back where we started with the band into the slower march or walking tempo. Need we say more? On we go again!

SUMMARY   Bars

1   Couples form a big circle around hall
2   Slow march tempo: eight steps
    forward, turning on the eighth
3   Slow march tempo: eight steps back,
    turning again on
    the eighth   (1–8)
4   Waltz tempo: pas-de-basque twice and
    two waltz turns   (1–8)
5   Waltz tempo: repeat 4   (9–16)
6   Reel tempo: pas-de-basque twice and
    two waltz turns   (1–8)
7   Reel tempo: repeat 6   (9–16)

THE GAY GORDONS

Well, we're almost through our second half of the programme—just two more to go before we face the chills of the night air and bed. Many a band leader in the days of the farm bothies has told me of getting back home in the wee sma' hours with just time to change the 'claes' and get straight into the byre or the stable to start a complete day's work. And you think I've tired you out with this small programme!

From the First World War, quick marches—devised area by area—became very popular in dance halls but many faded away. Here's one though that has retained its popularity throughout, just as the regiment to which it was attributed, The Pride of the North-East, The Gordon Highlanders.

The original tune has become known by the title of the dance but in fact that's not its correct title. I have seen the original manuscript by James Scott Skinner, the Strathspey King, with his distinctive scrawl dedicating this to a piping pal, a lad of thirty then, Pipe Major George S McLennan. It was composed in August 1915, on the fiddle maestro's seventy-second birthday and Skinner named it 'The Gordon Highlander's March'.

But to the dance. Again we start off facing round the room. The hold is called 'hand over shoulder', that is, I put my right hand on top of my partner's right shoulder and she stretches her arm up as I take hold of her right hand. She lifts her left hand to shoulder height and holds my left hand.

We walk four steps forward, half-turn and walk three steps (in reverse). Repeat that whole movement again—four forward, half-turn and walk three back. We should be back in our original positions.

I keep walking, with my right hand still holding my partner's right hand, while she turns ('birls') four times under my arm. We then take up waltz position and do three full turns. That's all nice and simple but very popular because of it.

Margaret tells me though that in recent years in the Lothians and Border areas, there has been a slight change in the latter part of this dance. Instead of the gent turning the lady four times under his arm, the couple join hands—gent's right and lady's left—and pas de basque out and in, repeat out and in, then take up waltz position and do three full turns. Quite simple and sometimes suits the dancers who perhaps can't turn because they get dizzy! Hey, I disapprove of that—that's no longer The Gay Gordons, but at least it's down here for the record!

SUMMARY   Bars

1	Couples form a big circle around hall	
2	'Hand over shoulder' hold, walk four steps forward, half-turn and walk three steps back	(1–8)
3	Repeat 2	
4	Gent walks forward, lady turns four times under gent's arm	(9–12)
5	Waltz three full turns	(13–16)

THE BROUN'S REEL

The Broun's Reel—deliberately chosen, as it was one of my late dad's favourites. The Broun's Reel or Duke of Perth (in some districts 'Clean Pease Strae') is to be found, in fact, in Book 1 of the RSCDS but here I get on the floor with Margaret for the last time to be put through my paces. This is a very energetic set dance with four couples per set, everyone having to keep alert throughout the dance.

The first couple is always the couple nearest the band. Gents are on the left in a straight line away from the band and ladies on right opposite their partners, making two straight lines of four.

Off we go then. The first couple turn each other with right hands, then cast off one, that is, the first lady goes behind the second lady, while the first man goes behind the second man. The second couple move to the top to make room. The first couple then meet in the middle of the set and turn each other by the left hand and finish in position for turning your corners.

At this point let me explain the corners in The Broun's Reel. The second gent is the first lady's first corner and the third gent is the first lady's second corner. For the first gent, his corners are the third and then the second lady. Simple enough, eh?

Continuing from where the first couple are in position for turning these corners, the lady steps and turns her first corner (second gent), while her partner proceeds to turn his first corner (third lady). All turn by the right hands.

The first couple meet naturally diagonally across in the middle of the set and turn each other by the left hand. Lady now proceeds to her second corner and turns gent with right hand, while her partner goes to his second corner and turns by the right hand. First couple meet again in the middle and turn twice by left hands.

Now for a change of pattern: I think I'll take up knitting—at least it would give me more time to think than I have here! Okay then, without a break in music, let's take the next movements. We'll call it section two though it's as one all the way through.

The first lady goes to her first corner (second gent), sets and turns him with both hands, then sets and turns her second corner (third gent). This is followed by the lady dancing a reel-of-three—weave in and out—with the two gentlemen. At the same time her partner (the first gent) should be dancing with the ladies thus: set and turn the third lady (his first corner) then set and turn the second lady (his second corner). He also does the reel-of-three with the two ladies. This first couple then dance over to their own lines, one place down having used up the complete thirty-two bars.

The second couple, now in first place, stand still through the next thirty-two bars while the first couple repeat the whole dance with the third and fourth couple.

After that little exercise, this time the first couple move down into the positions held by the fourth couple and the second couple get going now as first couple. The whole lot is repeated twice by each couple and if my mathematics are correct, we should all finish after eight times thirty-two bars.

SUMMARY
Bars

1	Sets of eight, comprising four couples	
2	First couple turn each other and cast off one on their own sides	(1–4)
3	First couple turn each other, finishing facing corners	(5–8)
4	First couple turn first corners, then turn each other	(9–12)
5	First couple repeat with second corners and turn each other finishing	(13–16)

71

facing first corners

6 First couple set and turn first
   corners with both hands, then set   (17–24)
   and turn second corners

7 Reel-of-three at both sides of
   the dance with respective corner
   partners, then first couple return   (25–32)
   to their own sides one place
   down

And there our ceilidh comes to a close. Ah, but does it? What did I say in the early chapters? We're elated, we're tired but our natural instinct is to reel again. Okay band? Auld Lang Syne and then before you put away these instruments, let's 'hae a final furl roon the fleer'.

Thanks to you all for dropping in past for the ceilidh.

> Noo I've sattled the score, an' the gig's at the door
> An' the shaltie is kittle to ca'
> Aye the langer we sit we're the sweirer to flit
> Sae it's time to be wearin' awa'.

A Cheery Guid-Nicht

Charles Murray, from Hamewith And Other Poems, before the days of more modern transportation. For the dancers there's nae change—and remember to take the music with you!

The Music

When Robbie Shepherd invited me to provide the music for this book I readily agreed but I admit to some reservations, as Robbie suggested that I should select for the dances tunes I would play myself.

I know that most dance bands and dancers have their own ideas of which tune is suitable for a particular dance and sometimes this is determined by the area where the dances are performed. The tunes I have selected are purely my own choice, tried and tested over the length and breadth of Scotland and here directed at the uninitiated musician as a guide.

Some of these dances have been imported into the Scottish Old-Time dance programme and it may well be that originally they were danced to a different type of tune, normally a folk tune from the country or area of origin, which would be adapted to suit the figure. It therefore seems right that where possible Scottish tunes should be used here in Scotland, as the Scot has a feel, when dancing, for the beat inherent in Scottish music and inevitably will feel comfortable while dancing to his own music regardless of the figure.

I was also asked to provide a list of alternative tunes which could be incorporated into a selection for each dance, as one tune is barely enough to sustain the duration of a dance figure which is likely to enjoy an encore. Any similar type of tune to the one I have suggested for each dance would suffice but I have provided a list of alternatives which are readily available to any musician.

The exceptions to this are perhaps The Swedish Masquerade, which has three different tempos incorporated within the figure and can present a problem when seeking a suitable alternative selection. However, I would suggest that an adaptation of Scottish tunes would be more than adequate.

And finally, The Lancers, better known as The Student Lancers. The selection for this dance should be played as per the music, as dancers normally know exactly where they are within the figure in relation to the tune and it would take a braver man than me to attempt changing this arrangement.

I hope my contribution to this book goes some way to providing many hours of enjoyment to dancers and musicians alike, and will help to keep alive some of the traditional Scottish Old-Time dances for future generations.

Jim Johnstone

THE GRAND MARCH
Garb of Old Gaul

Alternatives

Scotland Yet

Bonnie Gallowa'

Scotland the Brave

THE CIRCASSIAN CIRCLE
The Circassian Circle

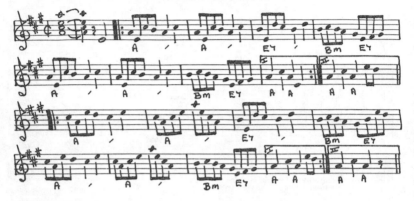

Alternatives

Lass o' Patie's Mill

Hey Johnnie Cope

Soldier's Joy

THE FRIENDLY WALTZ

Comrades

Four-bar intro.

Alternatives

I Belong to Glasgow

My Bonnie Lies Over the Ocean

I'll Be Your Sweetheart

THE DASHING WHITE SERGEANT

The Dashing White Sergeant

Alternatives

The Rose Tree

My Love She's But A Lassie Yet

Rakes of Mallow

THE BOSTON TWO-STEP

MacNamara's Band

Four-bar intro.

Alternatives

Household Brigade

Jeannie McCall

Six Twenty Two-Step

THE VIRGINIA REEL

Turkey in the Straw

Four-bar intro.

Alternatives

Yankee Doodle

Old MacDonald Had A Farm

I Come From Alabama

THE HIGHLAND SCHOTTISCHE

Orange and Blue

Two-bar intro.

Alternatives

Lad wi' the Plaidie

Louden's Bonnie Woods

John McAlpine

THE FOUR-HAND STAR
Waves of Tory

Alternatives

Come Let Us Dance and Sing

Davy Nick Nack

Babes in the Wood

THE PRIDE OF ERIN WALTZ

Believe Me If All Those Endearing Young Charms

Four-bar intro.

Alternatives

Homes of Donegal

Come Back to Erin

When Irish Eyes Are Smiling

THE EIGHTSOME REEL
Deil Amang the Tailors Fairy Dance

Tune 1 = 40 bars

Tunes 2, 3, 4, 5, 6, 7, 8 and 9 = 48 bars or 2 x 24 bars

Tune 10 = 40 bars

Alternatives

Wind That Shakes the Barley

High Road to Linton

The Breakdown

THE CALL O' THE PIPES

Barren Rocks of Aden

Four-bar intro.

Alternatives: Dornoch Links; Teribus; Sweet Maid
of Glendaruel

85

THE MISSISSIPPI DIP

On The Mississippi

Four-bar intro.

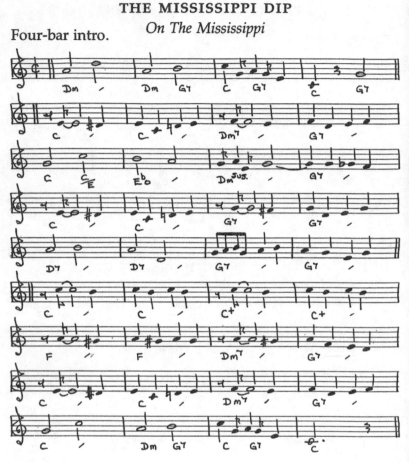

Alternatives

Swanee River

Robert E Lee

Poor Old Joe

THE EVA THREE-STEP

The Duke of Atholl

Four-bar intro.

Alternatives

The Scottish Horse

Midlothian Pipe Band

Bonnie Dundee

THE LOMOND WALTZ

Bonnie Bonnie Banks of Loch Lomond

Four-bar intro.

Alternatives

Comin' Thru' the Rye

Bless Them All

Neath the Shade of the Old Apple Tree

THE LANCERS

Figure 1

THE LANCERS

Figure 2

THE LANCERS

Figure 3

THE LANCERS

Figure 4

THE LANCERS

Figure 5

93

Figure 5 (continued)

Figure 5 (continued)

Figure 5 (continued)

THE ST BERNARD'S WALTZ

My Home

Four-bar intro.

Alternatives

The Cradle Song

Cuckoo Waltz

The Agnes Waltz

THE BRITANNIA TWO-STEP

The Quaker and His Wife

Four-bar intro.

Alternatives

Dovecote Park

Glendaruel Highlanders

Wade's Welcome to Inverness

THE SWEDISH MASQUERADE

Two-bar intro.

THE GAY GORDONS

Earl of Mansfield

Four-bar intro.

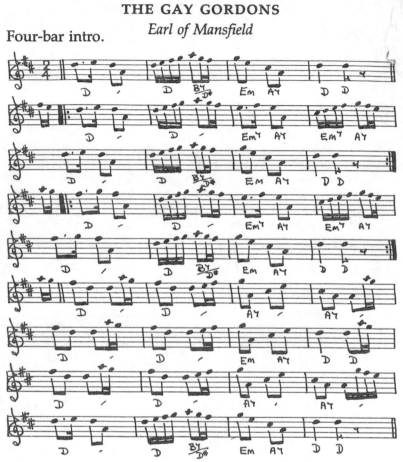

Alternatives

Cameron Highlanders

Campbell's Farewell to Red Castle

Invercauld